# I Didn't Know I Was Beautiful

*The Real and Raw Facts That Every Woman on The Planet Should Know*

Tara Tomlinson

Tanya R. Taylor

# TABLE OF CONTENTS


INTRODUCTION ..................................................... 6

CHAPTER ONE: Unhealthy Attachments

Misguided Compassion ......................................... 10

CHAPTER TWO

Releasing The Pain of The Past .......................... 16

CHAPTER THREE

A Fight with Depression ...................................... 25

CHAPTER FOUR

Outside Expectations ........................................... 34

CHAPTER FIVE: Constant Comparisons

The Impostor Syndrome ....................................... 39

CHAPTER SIX

True Beauty .......................................................... 48

CHAPTER SEVEN

The Perfect Date – Love or Hate? ....................... 53

CHAPTER EIGHT

If He Shows You Who He Is, Believe Him!........ 66

CHAPTER NINE

Embracing My Individuality................................ 72

CHAPTER TEN

Pick, Choose & Refuse ........................................ 81

CHAPTER ELEVEN

Staved for Affection ........................................... 88

CHAPTER TWELVE

Career-driven ..................................................... 94

CHAPTER THIRTEEN

True Sisterhood.................................................. 102

CHAPTER FOURTEEN

Avoiding Self-destructive Behavior ................... 110

CHAPTER FIFTEEN

Affirmations....................................................... 114

Conclusion ......................................................... 116

About The Authors ............................................ 120

Fiction Titles by Tanya R. Taylor..................... 124

*Suddenly, I realized why I'd put up with so much…*

*I didn't know I was beautiful.*

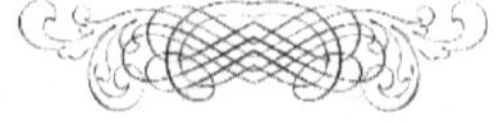

# INTRODUCTION

Our minds are *sacred databases*. Information is constantly being submitted, then stored or deleted. We cannot always control what enters our minds, but we do have the ability to determine what stays and what goes. What usually stay are memories from childhood or other events in life that were either difficult or pleasant. But how to "file them away" or compartmentalize them and also our perception of them generally determines the condition of our mental and emotional state; our perception of ourselves and others, what we allow as well as what we won't tolerate; how we interact with people around us and what our overall quality of life will be. That's a lot to consider, huh?

Well, it should be primarily because we all need to face the reality of how important our sacred databases are. You may wonder why, in this book, our minds are referred to as "sacred". In a nutshell, the health of our minds has a direct correlation to the quality of our life and perceived purpose of it or lack thereof. The way we think determines how we feel and ultimately what decisions we make and what actions we take. It's all connected. You may have heard or read about the power of our minds and how thoughts are like seeds that take root and affect our actions or sometimes inaction. Many women, in particular, are taught how to think, what to feel, what to choose based on others' expectations. We are trained to dress a certain way, speak a certain way, look a certain way and if we fail, we're not good enough or worthy of someone's love or affection. We seek approval from others instead of seeking our own. What do *we* want? What do *we* like? What matters to *us*? However, many times we avoid asking ourselves these questions because of the thoughts that were submitted and stored in our sacred databases. Yet, we also have the power to "delete" and we oftentimes don't select that option when we actually should. We can even "replace" the information that was once stored, and throughout this book, you'll be able to see how we can use these tools along with others to assist us in our quest to become the woman we were created to be.

What woman on this planet would not want to be self-assured, happy, confident, brave and living with a purpose? Not one. We all have an innate desire for those wonderful attributes, yet sometimes we struggle to achieve any of them which is reflected in the way we live our lives and what is attracted to us or hinders us. You might say that some are born with these qualities. That may be true, but it's also true that others work at it and realize that their weakness has turned to strength; their shyness has turned to boldness and confidence; their feelings of worthlessness and inferiority have been kicked to the curb and "replaced" with self-worth and self-assurance. Very few of us in life have had anything handed to us on a silver platter. We've had to work for what we wanted. Becoming the woman you were made to be is no different. It takes a willingness and determination—and with those two qualities, practically anything can be achieved.

In this book, you will be given many examples of characters who have faced similar issues to what you might have faced; their overall perception at the time they experienced them and the real and raw facts that every woman should know will follow each example. This is our gift to every woman who is walking this journey of life and who wants to ensure that each step counts and leads her to the quality of life she truly deserves.

# Chapter One

# UNHEALTHY ATTACHMENTS
## *MISGUIDED COMPASSION*

### *Sheila's story*

The summer of 1997 was a special time for me. I'd just landed a job at a local media company and had met a wonderful young man named Anthony—*Tony*, for short. He was three years older than me and I'd met him right after I'd graduated from high school. We had a beautiful courtship and he always treated me like a lady.

A year after we met, we were planning a small wedding, and six months later, officially tied the knot. Everything was perfect at first, then several months into our marriage, Tony started showing me a vastly different side of him that he'd managed to hide the entire year and a half we were dating. He became verbally abusive, criticizing everything I did. As far as he was concerned, I couldn't cook that well and could definitely use some lessons from his mother. I wasn't as "smart" as the women he worked with and could use some female assistance to teach me how to be more of a lady.

Soon feeling a great sense of inadequacy, I cried myself to sleep most nights and started to believe everything he'd said that basically summed up the idea that I just wasn't good enough.

What I didn't know when Tony and I were dating was that Tony came from a background that was as equally abusive and he had a demeaning mother who made him feel like he wasn't good enough either. He was only projecting upon me what had been projected onto him. Psychologically, he'd convinced himself that in order to be worthy as a man and as a human being, for that matter, he had to dominate someone else and make them feel the same way he'd felt growing up. He'd been horribly mistreated and now years later became the perpetrator. What was I to do? I couldn't just turn my back on him. At least that's what I thought.

A friend once tried to convince me to seek counseling without Tony. She felt I needed to work on myself first. Of course, I didn't take her advice; I've always felt that Tony could change and someday my marriage would get better. Twenty years went by and he only got worse. The verbal assaults turned to random physical attacks and I'd found myself buying dark sunglasses to hide the occasional bruises on my face.

Another five years went by and Tony was now a drunk and drug user. One night, he got mad that I didn't cook the "right dinner" for him and he became uncontrollably violent. I was sure he'd kill me, but that was the night that I grabbed the kitchen knife to defend myself...and I killed him.

It wasn't until I was arrested and charged with murder that I realized I'd made a serious mistake by making excuses for Tony's behavior instead of realizing it was not my job to change him, and that I didn't even have the power to. I could only change myself. It was then that I wished I'd gone to counseling years earlier to find out what it was that made me think it was okay to stay in an abusive relationship. If I'd taken the steps and done the work at the first sign of verbal abuse I'd suffered, I would have known it would not have been wrong of me to eject myself from such a toxic situation. But now it's too late; I cannot undo the past. I learned my lessons eventually, but not in time to prevent such a tragedy.

## The Raw Fact

For a long time, Sheila was subjected to abuse by the man she loved more than anything in the world. His baggage became her burden and she was emotionally crippled for many years. Through it all, her empathy for his past caused her to neglect her own mental, emotional and physical well-being. It robbed her of her strength, zest for life and she became another person. As verbal abuse turned to physical abuse, her life spiraled further downwards to the point of no return.

If you find yourself even in a remotely similar situation, don't let that be you. Don't allow your love for another person who abuses you to cause you your life or your freedom.

Some romantic relationships are unbalanced. Unbalanced in the sense that one partner loves the other far more than he or she loves him/herself and the partner takes full advantage of it. *Self-love* is vital to each and every relationship—not in an arrogant, selfish sort of manner, but in a healthy way. If you love yourself, then you will know what it is to love others the way you ought to and you will expect nothing less in return. You may sympathize with one's past, but will not *accept* it as an excuse for them to mistreat you. That's how you keep the scales balanced.

If that person's inner struggle becomes emotionally and physically draining to you, it's a toxic relationship and you should not be subjected to that. As an adult, your partner needs to seek the emotional help they need. If they refuse, you've got a decision to make for your own well-being. You cannot and I stress *cannot* change another human being. That power is not in your hands; you only have the power to change yourself. You can encourage and be that person's biggest fan, but they must be willing to do the work.

Don't be another *Sheila* who constantly made excuses because her love for her partner outweighed the love she had for herself. The scales were unbalanced and it eventually cost her her freedom.

# Chapter Two

## RELEASING THE PAIN OF THE PAST

*Julie's story*

I wondered when the time came if I'd miss her. All she ever did was made me feel ugly, inferior, and worthless. Although I knew I'd cry whenever she passed on, I wondered if those tears would be because I'd miss her or because I'd be reliving all the emotional pain she'd inflicted upon me ever since I knew myself. I'm a grown thirty-year-old woman now, but almost daily, hearing her voice and seeing her face is a constant reminder of all she'd put me through when I was an innocent, caring child who only wanted to love her and know that she was safe.

I wasn't her favorite—my only sibling, Bonnie, was and Mom never kept it a secret. Nothing I ever did was good enough for her. She often made snide remarks about my weight both at home and publicly. I was fairly chubby all throughout childhood and she was probably ashamed since no one else in the family was overweight. Bonnie was slim and beautiful and I was not. Mom even went as far as entering Bonnie in numerous beauty pageants and told me I wasn't thin enough to be in any. She constantly pointed out my flaws with a soft voice and a cunning smile. And many times as I sat alone in my bedroom while they all chatted and joked around in the living room, I wondered why I was ever born. Bonnie and I weren't close either. I got the impression earlier than I care to remember that she looked down on me because our mother obviously did.

My mother destroyed whatever hope there

was for me to be a happy, emotionally and mentally balanced individual. Now as an adult, I struggle daily to be *me*—who or whatever that is. Nobody knows, but I attempted suicide a few times—twice when I was a teenager and once after that. My husband, Marty, has no idea that the last time I tried to end it all, we were married and supposedly happy. Truth be told, we have a wonderful marriage; I just wasn't happy with myself. I'd never confided in him about any of those suicide attempts because I felt he'd look down on me and that's something I have a hard time dealing with. Mom had done a great deal of that and I knew I was scarred for life. So instead of coming out with it, I kept it all to myself.

Marty and I are about to celebrate fifteen years together and I've never told him about my deepest, darkest issues; I don't trust anyone enough to do so. The facade that I'd kept up for years that I "have it all together" is what keeps me sane, yet burdens me at the same time.

My husband could tell that Mom and I were

not close, although he never asked why. She and I talked almost every day, but he knew it was just a formality—something expected between a parent and a child to make sure each other were doing okay. There was no real connection—no bond and she has no idea how much I'm hurting because I can never tell her. I never stopped loving and caring about my mom, in spite of all the pain. Without a second thought, I would've died for her—just as I would have as a child. They say that love is all you need, but when it's reciprocated, that's when I say it's all you need.

Mom passed on and I never got to tell her how I felt. She left a lifetime of regret and a broken family, as Bonnie and I hardly ever kept in touch before or after Mom's passing. Her death was not the end, but rather the beginning.

I sort of regretted never telling her how I really felt regardless of what her reaction might have been. I always felt opening up to her would've been a waste of time since she never thought she was capable of any wrongdoing. But I started to think if only I had gotten the words out and expressed how I felt, I might have finally had the peace I'd sought after all my life. Now, it's too late. She's gone and I'm left with the scars in her wake.

**The Raw Fact**

Julie clearly struggled with emotional problems that started when she was just a child and she carried around those issues throughout her life. Anyone can sympathize with her situation and hope she'll get over it someday, but the truth is: emotional wounds are not easy to "get over" even after that person has matured as an adult. The issues that caused the sadness, self-doubt and depression must be confronted, and a good way to do so is by *expressing* them. In some situations, it's difficult to express them to the one that caused them, particularly if that person has moved away and you've lost contact or they've passed on like Julie's mom did before Julie ever got to tell her how she felt. Nevertheless, the act of expressing one's feelings is powerful because when it's done properly, it creates a "release".

Picture yourself holding some inflated balloons on strings outside on a fairly windy day and the magic that happens when you let go of the strings and release them into the air. You stand there watching as they go higher and higher and soon, there's no sight of them. Once you've released them, they don't turn around and come back to you. They're gone. That's the power of expression. Getting those words out that demonstrate what you're feeling (whether your perception is actually correct or incorrect) gives you a release—a profound opportunity to experience a freeing of the mind. The person's reaction to what you say is not as important as the peace that you'll eventually receive by expressing yourself.

Now that Julie's mom has passed on, how can she get her release? The answer is that her mother lives on inside her heart. So, whether or not they had a bond when her mom was alive, they're still connected. Julie has the power and opportunity to still express her feelings to her mom (not conjuring the dead, of course!) by simply finding a quiet space, taking a deep breath in and relating to her mom (as if she was right in front of her) what it is she feels in her heart about how she was treated, and leaving nothing out that must be said. If you believe in the afterlife, you may surmise there's a chance her mom, wherever she is, is listening and can now very clearly understand her daughter's feelings more than she would have if she was still alive. If you're not a believer, it's easy to accept that the very act of getting that burden off her chest would be life-changing.

Now back to the balloons.

After freeing yourself by means of verbally expressing the pain, it's now time to pay attention to the sky those balloons had floated up into. Picture the balloons now completely gone and no longer visible, and that perfectly clear sky is all that's left. The "sky" represents your new lease on life—a fresh start.

Smile and embrace it.

You are in charge of your life and you can decide to start on a new path of self-discovery and peace. Begin with affirmations (this is an important step in the achievement of any goal) and this will cause the effects of the negative words and actions of those who made you feel inferior to become smaller and smaller. As you speak positively, your thoughts and feelings will catch up to what you've said. And although you might not have believed those positive words when you first started speaking them, the more you persist the more they will become real to you.

Some examples of positive affirmations are:

*"I'm beautiful just the way I am and no one can convince me otherwise."*

*"I am worthy to be loved and respected."*

*"I am wonderful, talented and secure."*

*"If someone doesn't think I'm good enough, they have the issue and it's their loss and not mine."*

*"I will not allow other people's cruelty to cause me to become bitter."*

Affirmations you can say every day are included near the end of this book. I would suggest you choose three to say first thing in the morning and repeat at night before bedtime, depending upon the type of issue you're dealing with.

With just the right repetition of words and the power behind that simple act, you will be well on your way to becoming the best woman you can be; letting go of the past and embracing a wonderful future.

Chapter Three

# A FIGHT WITH DEPRESSION

***Tracy's story***

Growing up, I constantly felt a profound sadness—the kind that's so intense it starts to create physical pain. The funny thing is: I've had the perfect life—a great childhood, wonderful parents and lots of friends. Yet, somehow it never seemed like enough—like *I* was enough. And I've felt this way for as long as I can remember.

As a child, I assumed that everyone felt that way. I thought it was normal because it was *my* normal. It wasn't until junior high school that I learned about a word called *depression* and I remember it like it was yesterday.

It was a gloomy Thursday afternoon; the sun was nowhere in sight—only the sound of rain hitting against the pavement. I was sitting in my last class for the day which happened to be Counseling. I didn't like the subject, so never really paid attention like many of my peers. I thought the information was useless and the class a waste of my time. As I was sitting with a blank stare on my face, waiting for my teacher to arrive, my classmate Jonathan tapped me on the shoulder and asked if I was all right.

"Yeah, I'm good," I replied. "What's taking her so long?"

"She's out sick, so they're bringing in a guest to speak with us," he said.

Before I could reply, a lady I'd never seen before walked into our classroom. She was dressed in all black, wore heavy eye-liner and had a cross pendant on her necklace. For some reason, her Gothic appearance caught my attention.

"Hello, class. My name is Ms. Baker and I'm from the United Mental Health Association," she said. "Today, I'm going to be speaking to you about mental illness."

I was starting to zone out until she said the word *depression* and defined it. At that moment, my life changed forever and when I got home from school, I proceeded to do tons of research on the topic. I soon realized that I must've been suffering from depression all along and it's why I'd been feeling the way I felt. Almost all of the symptoms of depression I came across matched mine. For so long, I'd been feeling so weird and couldn't understand why, but now I finally did. Knowing what it was that I was grappling, somehow made it more real to me.

I also realized that not everybody felt the way I did, so I began to feel out of place—like I was an alien stuck on a strange, unfamiliar planet. I started to ditch school; push my loved ones away; was eating less and *black* became my favorite color. I didn't know how to make the pain stop, so I literally gave up and allowed my depression to consume me. It completely took over my mind and body to the point that I was no longer me—just an empty shell of a person. As the years went on, I became like a zombie; I felt so dead inside and like nothing mattered. Ultimately, it got so bad that I actually wished I was dead. I wanted to ask for help; to tell somebody how I felt, but I didn't know how. And I thought even if I did, they probably wouldn't have understood. I could be in a room full of people, but somehow, still feel completely alone. You'd think that someone with so much darkness would crave the light, but I didn't.

I was attracted to darkness and my dating life reflected this. I'm sure that no one was surprised because I'd failed at practically everything I did. I'd failed as a partner, a student, a daughter and a friend and I was sure there was nothing left for me. I had no control over anything in my life and was waiting around to die. I felt worthless.

At the age of nineteen, I developed an eating disorder called Bulimia. Maybe I did because the only thing I could control at the time was my eating, and perhaps, I just wanted to punish myself. Night after night, I knelt down with my head over the toilet seat. Every time I purged, I felt like a little bit of life left my body. I did it so often that I started to get sick; my body was slowly giving up on me. I could no longer keep food down and if, by chance, I did, I'd be in horrendous pain. The pain got so bad and my body so weak that I physically couldn't make myself throw up anymore. You might think this was a good thing, but I didn't. In my mind, it was just something else I'd failed at.

I didn't know what else to do, so I prayed. But instead of asking God to heal me physically and mentally, I asked Him to end my life. I was convinced there was no hope for me. I was in such a deep, dark, empty emotional pit and the light I once saw was completely gone.

On November 15th, 2017, my best friend died. I was so numb that I couldn't even cry at her funeral or bring myself to believe that she was really gone. Fourteen years of friendship and it ended in a split second. I thought for a while that it was a cruel joke.

I woke up one morning, weeks later, and the reality hit me that she was, in fact, dead and was never coming back. Strangely, it was also at that moment that something stirred inside of me. It was *hope*—hope that things could get better. I realized I didn't want to live like that anymore and wasn't sure that I wanted to die either. I knew I needed to change my life and from that point on, I gradually opened up to my loved ones about my problems and even agreed to go to therapy.

The first few sessions of therapy were hard. I felt uncomfortable, so I didn't speak much—just sat there while the therapist tried to get me to open up. She asked me questions, but also re-assured me that it was okay if I couldn't answer them. She knew I was uncomfortable and told me it was all right.

During the fifth session, I broke down in tears and told her everything. Her response was so caring and genuine. I started feeling more comfortable opening up to her and our sessions together became a safe place for me—a place without judgment.

As the weeks turned to months, I felt myself slowly getting better. The thoughts of wanting to die gradually faded until I didn't think about dying anymore. I also started to eat more and was getting stronger and healthier by working out. Learning how to control my mind drastically changed my life. I was taught how to shift my thoughts from something negative to something positive. I also understood that some of the people around me, the things I wore, and my surroundings affected my mental health. So, I avoided negative people; I chose to wear colors other than just black and I re-painted and redecorated my bedroom for a fresh start.

A year went by and I was very happy. Before then, I couldn't even remember what happiness felt like. It's crazy how the death of my best friend gave me a wake-up call. I truly think she's my guardian angel. She knew I was in a dark place and from Heaven, she helped bring me out of it.

**The Raw Fact**

Depression can affect any one of us. It doesn't affect just one race or gender—it doesn't discriminate. We don't choose depression, but if we're challenged with it, we can choose what to do about it. We can allow it to consume us like Tracy did in the beginning or we can fight it. The point here is to never give up. Don't push your loved ones away at the time you need them the most. Open up to them;

express your thoughts and feelings. They might be able to help you or steer you in the right direction.

Everyone needs help sometimes. The key to failing is thinking you can handle everything on your own. There is nothing you cannot overcome; just keep fighting and never lose hope. A brighter future lies ahead of you.

# Chapter Four

## OUTSIDE EXPECTATIONS

There's no simpler way for me to say it: **You must learn to master the art of not giving a rat's behind about other people's opinions of you.** When you can do that...*you've arrived!* Focusing your time and energy on what someone else thinks of you is like rejecting yourself and climbing into someone else's life (if you can imagine doing that). In other words, you quietly acknowledge that your own life's journey isn't as important as that of others, so you must exist in the box you've allowed them to put you in. That cannot be good enough for you... or is it?

Trying to live up to other people's expectations is a real chore. If you do it, you need to ask yourself why. Is it because you feel less important than others?

Parents have expectations for their children, which is natural. Every good parent wants the best in life for their child and tries to steer him or her in the right direction. They notice their child's special skills and abilities and help to guide them in ways where they can be developed and useful.

You want to study hard, show responsibility, be honest, courteous and treat others with respect. You also want to take sound advice from those who love and care about you, such as your parents and other family members.

When I speak of outside expectations, I'm referring to what falls outside of those healthy perimeters, such as people feeling the need to tell you what it is you must become in life when you feel a strong desire toward something else. Suggestions are fine, but everyone should be able to make up their own minds as to what they truly want out of life. A partner, for instance, should not dictate to the other how to dress. Again, suggestions are okay, but if you don't feel good about it, you should do what makes you feel comfortable. If someone said that you'd only be "accepted" if you joined a particular organization or spoke a certain way, you should think more highly of yourself than to give in to manipulation.

Think things through carefully; make up your own mind because at the end of the day, you're the one that has to live with yourself. You cannot live anyone else's life; just your own. So, get into the habit of feeling confident enough to make your own decisions and be woman enough to live with them.

I heard someone say years ago she wished she would've gone back to school because she always wanted to be a nurse. However, doing something totally different as a career, she was living up to someone else's expectations. Decades went by and she was much older and felt she'd never live her dream. It was sad to hear. I could not imagine wanting to have a particular career so desperately and not ever going after it. Outside expectations can be so damaging and have a life-long effect.

Some children were raised to think that girls must look a certain way, dress a certain way and act a certain way. And in some instances, the wrong concept had been drilled into their minds. Then when they couldn't live up to it, they felt inadequate and like a failure. When you were a child, your parents made decisions they felt were in your best interest, but as an adult, you're responsible for your own decisions. It's time to act like an adult. While never closing off your mind to good counsel, learn to trust yourself and follow the expectations you must have for your own life.

Aim to be a self-assured woman. Self-assured people don't constantly rely on others to tell them what to do. When they're faced with a situation, they carefully analyze it and make a decision they feel would be in their best interest or that of others. They're not sitting around second-guessing themselves because they're confident in themselves—which also makes them confident in their decisions. They're not moved by what others think or expect, but only by what they feel in their heart is the right move to make. In essence, self-assured people don't give a rat's behind about other people's opinion of them. Generally, they seem like happier people who know how to appreciate and enjoy life, and can even do so alone. They don't always need company or a partner and many of them are also very successful.

This should be your aim: to appreciate and enjoy life, and to live it to the fullest. It's difficult to make that happen when you're living up to other people's expectations instead of your own.

Chapter Five

## CONSTANT COMPARISONS/ THE IMPOSTOR SYNDROME

***Carly's story***

I watched Tina Mathers get award after award when we were in high school and guess what? She was also the teacher's pet. Not only was she the exact opposite of me in terms of appearance, she was physically fit; had slender arms (*unlike my bony ones*) and long, auburn hair that seemed easy to style—unlike my naturally frizzy hair that I struggled with endlessly. She must've had better genes and I was cursed.

My dad, a Czechoslovakian immigrant, always said that I was the "brains" of the family and that I'd be the first one in our family on both sides to go to college. He was counting on me getting a scholarship since I usually scored straight As. But Tina often scored way better. If I got twenty As in a semester, she got thirty and not only was she Ms. Claridge, our English teacher's favorite student, everyone loved her, even the Principal, Vice and other school administrators. They hardly ever noticed me. I wore thick, ugly glasses and looked like a toothpick in uniform.

Tina's family were all college-educated, pretty well-off and held top positions in many sectors of society. Everyone knew it. Her family was nothing like mine. We were between poor and middle-class and struggled to keep a roof over our heads and food in the cupboards. So many times, I wished I had Tina's life—that we could switch places. Maybe if she did, she wouldn't have seen the need to smile so much or be so bubbly all the time. I wondered if she could've ever survived in my world where the basic necessities never came easy.

With all that said, considering she and I were in the same class and in the top five of the so-called "smart students", she was pretty cool. She always hailed, although she never thought I was cool enough to actually bend a conversation with and that was fine with me. She was way out of my league anyway, so I could understand why a friendship between us would never happen. As for the other kids, they were sort of respectful towards me because they thought I was smart and where I come from, that was sort of a big deal even though I didn't really see how it was.

Apart from being so-called "smart', I literally had nothing going for me. I was fifteen-years-old and never had a boyfriend—much less a guy who'd ever shown any interest in me. I kinda had a thing for Carl Newry. He wasn't much of a looker, but he was confident, intelligent and I could tell he was going places. Carl never noticed me. He was clearly attracted to a pretty girl in school named Sandra who all the boys were crazy over. She wasn't so bright, but she had the looks that would probably take her anywhere she wanted to go in life. I hated her—not because of anything she did, but because she had what I didn't, just like Tina did.

When I finally graduated and went off to college, fulfilling my dad's greatest dream, I became a scientist in the field of Biochemistry and was able to land a job in a major city with a pretty good salary every month. I heard that Tina didn't do so well. She ended up dropping out of university to marry a well-known football player who treated her like crap. They had two kids. She eventually divorced, packed up the children and moved back home with her parents. Rumor was she couldn't hold down a job and was sort of a disgrace to her family since they all had done so well—cousins and all. Tina soon sank into depression and one day I heard on the news that she'd committed suicide. Apparently, she got hooked on prescription drugs and her family had been hiding that fact ever since she moved back home. I felt terrible for Tina and her family. She was the smartest one in our class; talented and loved by everyone, yet her life didn't turn out so well. Words can't describe how awful I felt. Why was I the one who did better? Why did I get to go to college and land the "perfect career", like my parents called it? I didn't deserve any of that. I wasn't worthy of it. For a long time, I battled with how a nobody like me could be looked up to by other people just because they thought I was smart.

Throughout my life, I couldn't help but wonder why anything good happened for me and I constantly compared myself with others. Because of that, I don't think I was ever truly fulfilled with what life offered, regardless of how great it supposedly was. At age thirty-six, I finally landed a boyfriend who was no *Carl*, in terms of brightness, but he was kind. After about a year of dating, I confided in him about how I never thought I felt worthy of anything good and that others around me were the ones who deserved my blessings. He seemed shocked that I felt that way, even about the prestigious award I ended up receiving for discovering a vaccine that would aid in the fight against a deadly disease. I was hailed as the youngest scientist to ever receive that award, but I couldn't understand what all the hype was about since I was only doing my job. Anyone else out there could've eventually come up with the same thing. At least, that's what I thought.

*Why me?* It was a question I never truly got an answer for. I never deserved anything good that ever happened to me because I was no one special. And nobody out there was able to convince me otherwise.

## The Raw Fact

Carly's perception of herself was clearly influenced by thoughts of unworthiness, which was no fault of her upbringing or family life. It was something she conceived by making constant comparisons of herself to others. She seemed more affected by the favoritism another student got over other students in her class, including herself. Why wasn't anyone ever able to convince her that she was as wonderful as they perceived her to be—her parents, her peers, her colleagues and even her boyfriend? What underlying thought process had driven her to deem herself unworthy of anything good even when she was a child?

Carly's tendency to compare herself to others instead of embracing what she had within herself, specifically the skills and talents she had been blessed with, is what formed her skewed perception and kept it that way throughout her life even into adulthood. She was largely unaffected by her father's praise and that of those around her because she was consistently looking **"from the outside in"** instead of **"from the inside out"**. Consequently, she never truly enjoyed her many accomplishments and thought she didn't deserve them.

That is why learning to appreciate who you are and becoming comfortable in your own skin, regardless of your physical appearance is so vital to a woman's mental health. You must train your sacred database to look from the inside out and not the other way around.

When you look from the inside out, you tend to see and appreciate the talents you've been blessed with and utilize them to help yourself and others along life's journey. You embrace the thought that everyone has their own gifts and their own journey to travel. And your focus will be on living your own life and viewing yourself in the light that you are capable and *deserving* of achieving great things with what you've been blessed with.

Don't mistreat yourself by focusing on other peoples' talents and accomplishments, and comparing theirs to yours. Appreciating what's inside of you is important for your mental and emotional well-being. Cherish your uniqueness and perceive it as something wonderful. Not everyone is going to look like a supermodel (and you do know that so-called look is generally "manufactured" anyway, right?), but perception is everything. Having the right perception of yourself, especially if you are struggling in this area, starts by looking past your flaws, and focusing on those qualities you have inside that make you the wonderful, beautiful woman that you truly are. Affirm yourself. Say things like: "I'm really gorgeous!"; "I'm smart in my own way" (even if you're not book smart); "I love what I see (even if you don't like the bulges, chubbiness, or the skinniness – say it anyway!). Before long, you will start to see and appreciate the new you—a woman deserving of great things just like every other woman out there.

## Chapter Six

## TRUE BEAUTY

They say that beauty is only skin deep. Basically, it means that true beauty goes beyond one's physical appearance. A person may be gorgeous on the outside, but ugly on the inside and obviously, that's not a good thing.

People these days pay so much attention to what's being publicized out there as beauty. You see the anorexic-looking models, narrow faces and flawless skin and you think that's how a woman is supposed to look. It's the reason so many young girls are starving themselves daily and becoming anorexic or bulimic in order to achieve the advertised "cosmetic version of beauty". If only these young people can ask some of those same models what they go through to maintain their weight and supposedly "flawless features", they'd understand that what they may be aiming for might not be worthwhile to them.

Why do you think there's a natural instinct for various people in the world to be attracted to different types of people? It's because beauty comes in all colors, shapes and sizes. One person's definition of a beautiful woman may be tall, thin and having narrow features, while someone else's might be short, plump and more rounded features. Why people make such an effort to look like someone else makes absolutely no sense! The way you are right now—regardless of your height, shape or size—is someone's definition of beautiful, and it needs to be your definition too.

Do you have curves in more places than you'd like? Learn to view those curves as beautiful, simply because they are a part of your physical body.

If you learn to hate your own body, there's a possibility that you won't think much of yourself—*the real you* who lives inside of it. That becomes a very dangerous situation.

Some women have literally self-destructed because they are not comfortable in their own skin. They judge themselves harshly, based on their perception of what they see in the mirror. And sadly, their perception is based primarily on someone else's views and ideas. This is indeed a tragedy. Imagine if you were comfortable in your skin. Your focus would not be constantly on your appearance, but on other things you would be able to better focus on like an education, choosing a great career—something you'd be good at, building good, healthy relationships, relaxing and having fun as often as you should. If you are obsessed with your appearance, you can only see in a skewed manner; you cannot see the big picture.

If you are overweight and would prefer to lose weight in order to be healthy and look your best, that's a wise choice. But do it for yourself—not because it's more "socially acceptable". It's crucial that whatever decisions you make concerning your body are influenced by your own perception and not by warped outside ideas that you've made your own. Remember that beauty is not one model. There are so many versions that adequately fit the description. If you aren't overweight, but don't think you have a pretty face, think about why it is you can look at yourself and don't feel pretty. Is it because someone said you were "plain" or "ugly"? If so, who are they to decide what pretty or beautiful is?

The fact that you were made the way you were means that the Creator saw you as beautiful. How tragic for you not to see yourself the same way! Please learn to tell yourself that you are beautiful whether or not you believe it. Practice makes perfect. If you tell yourself you are pretty or you are beautiful often enough, you will believe it one day and when that day comes, no one else will be able to convince you otherwise. There is nothing like believing in yourself. That person who thinks you're unattractive or ugly didn't create you, so their opinion is null and void. The quicker you accept that fact, the better your life will be; the happier you will find yourself from day to day and you'd be able to look ahead and plan for a fabulous future that is certainly within reach.

Do not be obsessed with your physical appearance. *The real you*—your true beauty lies within and your self-confidence will cause everyone around you to see it whether they ever admit it or not. That's not your concern. Your concern and focus must be on your inner qualities and attributes while you appreciate and embrace the physical part of you. **Love yourself**—every part of you—and don't believe the naysayers. Remember that empty barrels make the most noise. Keep your poise; believe in yourself; get comfortable in your own skin because when you are, there's not a soul out there powerful enough to make you feel badly about yourself!

<u>Chapter Seven</u>

## THE PERFECT DATE - LOVE OR HATE?

***Chandra's story***

Jake was the perfect guy—my Prince Charming. He was wonderful, kind, gentle; everything I thought he would be and more. We attended the same school and he was two years my senior. He must've felt my constant stare from the bleachers while I watched him play football after school. And noticed the way I shyly smiled at him when he walked over to claim his gym bag after a competitive game. He always returned a soft smile my way, not knowing that I stayed behind every time not just to watch our school team put to shame the visiting team, but to watch him play. I was hopelessly in love; could barely concentrate in class because Jake Phillips was constantly on my mind.

I seriously wondered if he even gave me a second thought and if that soft smile he sent my way was only out of courtesy that he'd offer to anyone. I wasn't sure—until the day came when he approached me after one of the games and made "small talk". If only you could've heard his voice! It was enough to take my breath away.

Up until I met Jake, I must admit, I was pretty confident in myself. I thought I was pretty enough to attract most guys, but wasn't so sure I'd ever be able to get Jake's attention. He was practically every girl in my school's dream and had the features of a young Greek god. Even with the level of confidence I had, I was doubtful, yet hopeful that he'd ever give me the time of day.

To my delight, coming over to me at the bleachers became a regular routine for Jake. He'd sit next to me and we'd chat for about twenty minutes before Mom came to pick me up. I would call her a few minutes before the game would end so she'd be on her way.

"I never knew you liked football," she commented on one occasion.

"I didn't either!" I said.

Before long, Jake asked me out on a date. Yes! A real date! I was sooooo excited, I could barely breathe for days on end just thinking about it! It was that big of a deal. He said he'd take me to his uncle's restaurant downtown and it turned out to be the one my mom and her co-workers regularly went to for lunch. Mom loved the place and said he'd made a good choice.

I dolled up that Saturday evening and had literally spent hours getting my hair and nails done. Mom and I even went shopping for a new outfit for me. I was beaming from ear to ear and she wanted nothing more than to see me happy.

Our first date was perfect; I even got to meet Jake's Uncle Tony and two of his cousins. They were delightful and I thought they liked me. Of course, that was just a first impression, but to me, everything seemed to flow smoothly. After dinner, we parked at the fort which overlooked the city and just looked on at the dazzling array of lights. We even had our first kiss that night in the car and I knew right then and there that I was hooked. It was my very first romantic kiss ever.

Over the course of three months, Jake and I spent most of our free time together. After a while, Mom and Dad became concerned because they thought I was neglecting my studies by being in a relationship with Jake. Admittedly, I wasn't paying as much attention to school work as I had been, but I still always managed to get good grades. So it wasn't like I'd chosen our relationship at the expense of my education.

Mom liked Jake, but Dad hadn't really warmed up to him and I could feel the tension in the air whenever Jake came over. I tried talking to Dad about it once, but he was dismissive of it, saying he had no problem with the guy other than the fact that he was taking up too much of my time. Education was everything to Dad. He didn't get to finish high school because he was forced by his folks to quit when he was senior in order to work full-time and help take care of the family. He had years of struggle before he got his GED, then eventually went to community college and got his Accounting degree. I knew Dad was only reacting to Jake the way he was out of concern, but I wished they were close. And that was important to me because in my mind, I was sure Jake would be my husband someday.

I learned at our eighth month mark that my hopes of a long-lasting love affair with Jake was nothing but a fantasy. I'd seen the signs at least a couple of months before that as he was backing off and making constant excuses as to why we couldn't meet up on the weekends anymore. He suddenly had "other things to do". I couldn't understand the switch. He was so in love with me the whole while (at least that's what I thought), then all of a sudden, he was ignoring me. In the locker room after one of his football games, I approached him and demanded an explanation for the cold shoulder he was giving me. I'd never forget what he said to me: "It's time to wake up from that fairy-tale dream you've been having, Chandra. I'm not in love with you. I've been using you because you're so easy."

He actually had a smirk on his face when he said it. I couldn't believe my ears. With tears welling in my eyes, I ran out of there and behind one of the buildings, and called Mom to pick me up. I was a complete mess when she finally pulled up and I had to stop her from going to find Jake. She was so angry; she wanted to kill him for breaking my heart.

That evening after Dad found out, he came into my room and told me it was okay and that I'd forget about the jerk before I even knew it. I didn't believe it though. How could I ever forget about the love of my life – my first love? Dad couldn't be right about that. Jake was my world and without him, life was not worth living.

I'd made the decision days before I actually carried it out. After the break up, I'd missed two days of school before my parents practically forced me out the door. I soon had to figure out how to cope with still attending the same school as Jake and having to see him from time to time.

For a few weeks, I thought I was getting stronger, although nowhere near where I needed to be in order to feel like myself again. Then I noticed Jake was hanging out with Becky, a popular girl in my class. They obviously had a thing going. It was days after that that I made the decision to kill myself. I felt worthless, unloved and wanted nothing more than for the nightmare I was living to be over. I couldn't do it anymore.

I told my parents that Wednesday morning that I wasn't feeling well and was going to stay home from school. They thought maybe I'd come down with a cold or something, so they secured the house as they were leaving for work. After they left, I took the small bottle of my dad's prescription pills out of his medicine cabinet and went to my room. He'd just filled that prescription the week before.

Drenched in tears, all alone in the house, I swallowed the entire bottle of pills and lay back on my bed. I stared blankly at the ceiling thinking about how worthless I was because I wasn't good enough for Jake to love and to want to stay with me. Our relationship was a lie and I was better off dead. Those thoughts were overwhelming and I struggled with them from the day he broke up with me. I'm not that strong like other girls were who'd had their hearts broken.

After several minutes, I became very lightheaded and almost felt like I was floating out of my body. I knew the end was near and although I loved my parents and knew the decision I'd made would destroy them, I knew no other way. As I drifted quietly away, I soon heard the jingling of keys at the front door. I was too weak to respond for at any moment, I'd be gone.

I woke up in the hospital and later found out my dad had forgotten his briefcase the day I'd swallowed the pills and had to return home for it. He found me unconscious, but had arrived in the nick of time. The doctor told my parents that if I hadn't arrived at the hospital when I did, I would've been dead.

After I was discharged from the hospital, I saw the pain on my parents' faces and what I'd put them through, and I came to regret what I'd done. I still was hurt by Jake's rejection of me, but after counseling, I soon was able to see the picture of life more clearly and realized no boy—*no one* was worth me taking my own life. I realized what a mistake it would've been for me to end my life, which was a precious gift given to me—while he went on living his. They say hindsight is 20/20. For me, it was.

That was many years ago. I went on to marry the love of my life and we have two wonderful adult-children. I often think about how I would've missed out on so much if I had died that day when I was just sixteen-years-old. I wouldn't have experienced the happy times that came later; the life lessons and the good that came out of them. I cherish my life now and those who love me, and have never again allowed sorrow or betrayal to sink me far enough into depression where thoughts of suicide reside. I was given a second chance, unlike many who've gone before me, and I'm grateful to say I made the most of it.

## The Raw Fact

Do you remember the butterflies you felt in your stomach when you met that special someone? I do.

What about losing your first love? I'm sure many of us have dealt with that pain.

Whether it's your first love or fifth, we know that failed romantic relationships can take a toll on a person's mental health and have sometimes led to acts of suicide.

Unfortunately. it's relatively easy to sink into depression after losing someone you loved or *thought* you loved. You're left feeling empty, worthless, and extremely sad. You can't quite think as clearly as you should and your mind starts harboring unhealthy thoughts that you feel you have no control of. The truth is: You *do* have control of those thoughts, even in your misery. The problem is you're so disheartened that you don't feel strong enough to arrest them. Heartache comes and goes and it's important to keep in mind that just as it appeared, at some point, it will leave. A failed love affair isn't something that should rob you of your joy forever. It's a part of traveling this journey called *life*.

What would be ideal is if you entered all relationships with the thought that it would be nice if those people are meant to stay in your life, but if not, you accept the possibility that their departure was necessary for you to get where you need to be in your journey. Not everyone you meet in your life is meant to stay. Some only arrive to serve a purpose that you can learn from which would aid you further down the road, while others were meant to stay. If you keep that perspective, you will more easily accept whatever comes your way. And although parting ways and the manner in which you do might be difficult, you'd know in your heart of hearts—in some way you'll see later on— that it was necessary.

Thankfully, Chandra is able to look back and see how blessed she's been to continue her life without Jake. She'd never forget the experience, but it has no power over her and cannot hinder her because she's tucked it away as a mere *life experience*.

# Chapter Eight

## IF HE SHOWS YOU WHO HE IS, BELIEVE HIM!

I highly recommend the book _How To Have A Loving Marriage With An Unlovable Spouse by J.S. Wright._ Although it's geared towards folks that find themselves in less than ideal romantic relationships that could have spanned years, it also covers topics such as: Dating, How Opposites Attract, Understanding the "Baggage Phenomenon" and so much more. I thought the additional advice on dating, in particular, would be quite useful here.

So many times, we, as women, are fortunate to have seen the signs during the dating period and because we're head over heels in love or have this crazy notion that we can "change" a grown man, we ignore the signs and settle. And settling sometimes causes us a lifetime of pain.

Below is an excerpt you might find interesting if you are a woman who has settled or one who doesn't intend to:

*Consider this—If you dressed up nicely for your first, second, third or fourth date and the guy never once said how lovely you looked or never paid you any compliments at all, would you still be interested in pursuing a more serious relationship with him? What if he was very handsome, intelligent or had a strong sex appeal, yet he didn't seem to notice anything that was worth complimenting you for?*

*Some of you would say, "I don't care how good-looking he is, I'd have to leave that one alone!" You might have the opinion that basically what you see is what you get and that's a good way to look at it. But there are others who would blatantly "ignore" the tell-tale signs that the guy isn't going to be the type of man to satisfy their emotional needs. They're smitten by him and are convinced that once they get a good grip on him and he falls madly in love, later on he'll change and become the Prince Charming every girl dreams of. This kind of woman feels she has the magic touch to create a new, loving, sweet, affectionate man. Keep dreaming, sister!*

*That is, undoubtedly, one of the first serious mistakes women tend to make – many of us believe we can "tame" a man and mold him into what we want him to be. Wake up! He's not a toy. He's a human being with feelings, emotions and a history that you may or may not be privy to. He's not a puppet on a string and shouldn't be treated as such with sheer manipulation to achieve a goal we've set for our lives. If you've got a pretty sharp guy there in terms of intelligence who also has a stubborn streak and can see through what you're trying to do, the only person who will be changing is you because a man like that will put up a resistance like you won't believe.*

*So, what's the bottom line here? PAY ATTENTION TO THE EARLY SIGNS. Don't ignore or deny his mannerisms and behavior. Instead, think about what he's showing you and try not to think with your heart all the time. You've got to use your brain (common sense) because therein lies reason and logic. If a man shows you very little interest from the onset of the relationship, there's a huge chance that what you get moving forward won't be much more than he's already showing you outright. Actually, it could get worse! You then have to decide if that type of behavior/attitude is something you can easily tolerate going forward for perhaps - ten, fifteen, twenty or thirty more years.*

*Men also meet women who are emotionally unavailable – who have a chip on their shoulders and feel like the world owes them something. Brothers, be very selective of the woman you choose as a wife. If she is loving, honest, and kind towards not just you, but others as well, you've got a jewel there. Treat her right and don't mess it up! And vice-versa for the woman who has a guy who takes real interest in her; is kind, loving and affectionate. Don't make the mistake of taking his kindness for weakness; you may live to regret that when you see he's moved on to someone else who truly appreciates him.*

*If someone shows you who they are... BELIEVE THEM! It's that simple. Do not make excuses. You're not that person's mother and he or she is no longer a child. If someone you're interested in developing a meaningful relationship with has deep-seated emotional issues, be aware that he cannot satisfy your emotional needs because he himself is struggling to come to terms with his own.*

*You don't want half of a person – you want the whole,*

*fully functioning individual as your partner in life.*


*(From the book: 'How To Have a Loving Marriage With An Unlovable Spouse' – available at Amazon. Used with permission.)*

Chapter Nine

**EMBRACING MY INDIVIDUALITY**

***Heather's story***

Have you ever been teased or picked on for being "different"? I surely was. It started when I was in grade school, and as much as my parents loved me and showed me they did every day, there was nothing they could do about the derogatory remarks and cruel jokes that came at me when I wasn't with them. See, I was born with a disability. When my mother was giving birth to me, the doctor pulled my leg a bit too forcefully which injured it and caused me to walk with a pronounced limp. My parents sued the hospital and won, but in the end, after seeking the help of experts, they were told there was nothing they could do and that I would have to walk with a limp for the rest of my life.

As a toddler, it took me longer than most to learn how to walk. And when I did, I noticed I had this wobble that came along with it. To me, at the time, it was natural. However, as I grew older, I recognized that no one else was walking quite like me.

When I was in third grade is when, to my recollection, the teasing started. I'd just transferred to a new school and there was a boy named Mike who took it upon himself to point at my legs and laugh while we were all out to P.E. one afternoon. I was running with a group of other students and for obvious reasons, he singled me out. Then all the other children started laughing and I quickly slowed down, then stopped altogether. Mrs. Dawkins, our P.E. teacher told them to knock it off, but she couldn't completely stop the snickering—the damage had already been done.

I escaped to the restroom afterwards, locked myself in a cubicle and cried. From that day forward, it became a regular routine. Of course, I wasn't the only kid being made fun of. The chubby ones like Tommy Whittaker and those who were remarkably thin like Alice Johnson were also the brunt of jokes. Let alone the kids whose vision wasn't the best and who had to wear thick eyeglasses.

Mike was relentless in his teasing, taking a shot at me every chance he got. And a number of other kids around school caught on to it and figured they'd have more "fun" if they joined in. I wasn't the type to laugh it off and pretend I wasn't hurt. I'm sure it showed in my face every time it happened how hurt I was. But they didn't care; they were just kids who weren't very nice.

After school when my dad picked me up and asked me if I had a good day, I'd lie and say "It was okay,". He and Mom must've figured something was going on with me because a few months later on Report Card Day, Mom and Dad spoke with my homeroom teacher Mrs. Isaacs who told them she'd witnessed some teasing from time to time and had punished Mike for it. I'll never forget the look in their eyes after they'd learned what I was going through at school. I knew they felt helpless and probably even guilty for my plight, but when they spoke with me about it, I told them neither Mike, nor any of the other children got to me. I lied because I didn't want them to worry about me.

After I went on to middle school and then high school, there was always someone who had fun at my expense. By the time I was sixteen, I'd pretty much learned to endure it. Sure, I still escaped to the restroom sometimes to cry alone in a cubicle, but I was stronger than I was when I was in grade school. I'd convinced myself years earlier that one day I'll show them and they'd be sorry for how they treated me.

Without the love and support of my parents, I doubt I would've been so strong. I did what they wanted me to do which was to concentrate on my lessons and focus on the future. I always wanted to be a mechanical engineer. Most girls my age in my school didn't seem the least bit interested in such a career, but I knew that was what I was meant to be. I loved "inventing" things and fixing things, even though the one thing I wish I could fix wasn't something that I, in fact, could—my leg. Nevertheless, I was determined to go to college and embark upon a career I was sure I'd love.

It was at that time that I learned to embrace my individuality. I couldn't change who I was nor my disability, but I could learn to look at it in a way I never quite did before. The way I walked made me different from others around me and I started to think that maybe being "different" wasn't so bad. I actually questioned myself: *Am I my legs or my body? Am I the way that I walk? Does my disability make me less special than everyone else who doesn't have one?* The answer to all of the above came quickly and it was a resounding *No!* I realized that my body is a shell—a vehicle that the real me lives in. And just because I couldn't do so well some of the things other kids could, didn't mean they were better than I was. I knew my qualities—that I was kind and considerate, and I liked that about myself. I embraced who I was (disability and all) and that made all the difference in my life.

I graduated from high school and went on to university. Within five years I had my degree and completed the job training I needed in order to become certified. I must admit that getting through university was easier than all the other schools combined. I don't remember being teased even once after I went off. Even so, the scars were there and the damage had already been done after so many years of enduring relentless teasing and crying many tears. It was tough enough getting around more slowly than everyone else because of my disability, but the emotional pain inflicted upon me through no fault of my own, had made life a thousand times worse for me.

I hated what that kid, Mike, and the others had put me through and as an adult felt sorry for the kid in me who could do nothing about it. It was when I got to university that I realized I had to forgive them all and let it go. Although I hadn't seen them for a long time and didn't care to, I verbalized my forgiveness in the privacy of my dorm room, knowing that one day they'd all realize how wrong they were. From that day forward, I was a happier person and life presented many opportunities for me as a mechanical engineer in the town where I'd grown up.

Years later, I saw Mike at a trade show we both attended for the companies we worked for. He was a purchasing agent and had apparently done well, except for having some major losses in life that I'd heard about through the grapevine. He hailed from about ten feet away, but never approached me even to apologize for his actions as a kid.

But I didn't need his apology.

I was already at peace with him and myself because regardless of what he or others thought or did to me and how they didn't accept me for who I was, I accepted myself and that's all that mattered. He didn't look so happy from what I could tell, but I was.

## The Raw Fact

Heather struggled with constant emotional and mental abuse because of her apparent disability. However, as a teenager, she learned to appreciate what it was that made her "different" and learned to love herself just the same. She embraced who she was and never looked back. This is a lesson for every child out there who has ever been teased or bullied. There's nothing wrong with being different. The truth is that none of us are the same; we're all unique anyway.

Heather's story is also a lesson for women who have been rejected by others due to their social status; not being a part of a clique or have been bypassed for job promotions simply because they are women. Just keep doing your best and improving yourself, and one day you'll see the rewards.

Everyone has their challenges, but learning how to deal with them is what counts in the long run. Embracing your individuality is what gets you on the road to success. Life is unfair and good people are sometimes overlooked and taken advantage of, but it doesn't mean that you should shrink to the floor with feelings of inferiority, thinking less of yourself because of how you were treated. If Heather didn't have the right outlook on life, she wouldn't have ultimately won. You can win too!

# Chapter Ten

# PICK, CHOOSE & REFUSE

As a woman, you want to put and *keep* yourself in the position where you can pick, choose and refuse. If you're single, you definitely don't want to make the mistake of having it any other way.

Whether you realize it or not, people generally can sense your confidence or timidity. And those with bad intentions may decide to try and take advantage of your apparent weaknesses.

As it applies to dating, oftentimes when the whirlwind courtship is over and the wild bubbly feelings have settled down, some partners don't put forth the effort needed to nurture their relationship. In other words, they figure they've got you where they want you and it's a done deal.

While you cannot possibly control anyone's actions, you shouldn't be slack in making it clear about what your expectations are.

When a person becomes so carefree in a relationship where he feels "safe" that you're going nowhere—no matter what—it spells major trouble for the relationship. And overtime, your unhappiness may lead to wrong and unhealthy decisions that you might live to regret.

Many times women have settled for whatever came after the first few months of dating. They have inadvertently given their partner the impression that he no longer needs to put forth the effort he willingly did when they first met because she loves him too much to ever leave him. If you've found yourself in this situation, ask yourself this question: Has your self-worth declined just because you've found yourself a boyfriend or tied the marital knot?

Hopefully not!

Some partners end up paying less attention to their significant other and more to their friends, hobbies, etc. – or in more severe cases, completely loses the respect they once had for the person they've made a lifelong commitment to.

Tell me: Should respect go out the door?

Absolutely not!

That's why it's very important to work on yourself—build your self-esteem and confidence, then your very *presence* will demand respect from those around you, particularly those you've allowed to be a part of your life. I stated your "presence" for a significant reason. If you carry yourself properly, you won't feel the need to shout everywhere you go and from the roof-tops that everyone far and near must respect you. Your very presence will speak to that end.

My emphasis here is not in the way you dress or what your social status is. Once you wear clean clothes and practice good hygiene, that takes care of the physical aspect. More importantly is the psyche—the part of you that has nothing to do with physical appearance. It's the spiritual and emotional side of you that needs to be at peace and secure within itself, and it will give off an invisible aura without any major effort on your part. This is the position you want to be in. It's a comfortable one that isn't always on the battlefield trying to convince others that you're worthy of respect and honor. It becomes something that's naturally "sensed" or picked up on.

Even so, does it mean that you won't come across uncouth and insolent people from time to time who feel the need to "test" you? No, it doesn't. It means that you will do what is within your power to live decently, behave appropriately, and care for yourself in such a manner that no one in their right mind would think that you are unworthy of common courtesy and respect. Those that do will learn *from you* what it means to be a lady and to be dignified. Dignified in the sense that you know not every battle is worth the fight (which means you choose them wisely). Dignified in the sense that won't get into a nasty verbal assault with someone who disrespected or mistreated you or even worse an all-out brawl. Dignified in the sense that you know how to find the door and walk away from trouble.

You have the power to pick, choose and refuse who your company will be—whether it's a romantic relationship or a regular friendship. No relationship can thrive where there is a lack of admiration and mutual respect.

Love yourself enough to select the right individuals for your inner circle—those who genuinely care about you and support you. Pick your friends, choose your company, and refuse or reject those who are apt to mistreating others (because they will mistreat you too someday. It's just a matter of time).

If you are in a relationship where you've slackened your expectations of proper and decent treatment over time, you need to remind yourself, first of all, of what you deserve and expected when you first signed up, and if you must, remind your partner. Let me be clear: I'm not suggesting you run off whenever there's a problem or disagreement. Even the most ideal relationships have their share of arguments. You can disagree without making it a habit of demeaning the other person or calling them outside of their name. It sets the stage for verbal and emotional abuse, and bit by bit the ill-treatment eats away at the soul until you feel you have no strength left to fight. But you shouldn't have to constantly fight for respect and that's my point. It should be readily reciprocated at all levels and stages of your relationship. If it doesn't, maybe you need to ask yourself what it is you truly want out of life.

I would never advise anyone to simply settle for a relationship or friendship that is emotionally draining or toxic. It's not healthy. You are a lady; you are a queen, so you should keep yourself in a position to be able to pick, choose and refuse. The options are there and the power at your fingertips.

# Chapter Eleven

## STARVED FOR AFFECTION

***Michelle's story***

I once asked a friend how her childhood was. She immediately said, "Great!", then gave me all these examples of how it was awesome. She said that she and her family traveled a lot and when on outings, sang silly songs in the car. She talked about how very close they were. When she was done explaining, she asked me how my childhood was. I just stared at her for a while with a confused look on my face. I have no idea why I didn't expect her to ask after I had asked her. It's just the polite thing to do.

Eventually, I said, "It was okay", then quickly changed the subject. I mean…what was I supposed to tell her? Was I supposed to say that it was awful? Then give her examples of how awful it truly was? Like the time I watched my dad break a vase over my mom's head or the time when my mom called me stupid and worthless for dropping a glass of milk? I don't really know how to answer those types of questions other than by saying, "It was okay". Most of the time people don't even care; they're only asking to be nice anyway.

Growing up, I was really confused about what love was. In school, we were taught it was kind, but the "love" I saw at home was my dad beating my mom, then saying *sorry*. I was also taught that love is forgiving, so saying "sorry" made it okay, right?

When I started dating, I went out with guys that were exactly like my father. Dad was the only male figure in my life, so to some degree I admired him.

I know what you're thinking…

*Yeah, well…that was stupid right?*

To be honest, it was, but at that time it felt right to me. It also led me to the ER five times because my boyfriends beat me. But they always did come back and apologize, so I forgave them. They felt badly about it, so they must've loved me—at least that's what I thought.

One time, my boyfriend Jackson broke three of my ribs and shoved my head into a glass table in the living room. I was in such bad shape that the doctors had to put me under a medically-induced coma where I remained for three months. When I woke up, I was a completely different person.

While I was under, I had vivid nightmares of Jackson killing me; a scenario that played over and over again—at least twenty times in twenty different ways. Those nightmares served as my wake-up call and I knew if I remained in that toxic relationship, it would be the death of me. I decided I needed to be alone, but making that decision was the hardest thing I'd ever done. I wasn't used to being by myself. I always had a boyfriend and if we happened to break up, I'd be with a new guy practically days later. I was painfully aware that if I had to be alone, I'd have to be alone with my thoughts as well, yet that's precisely what I needed.

During those moments of solitude, I realized that I had no idea who I was. I didn't know my favorite color, my favorite food, my favorite movie or even how tall I was. I'd been so busy getting to know other people that I never made an effort to get to know myself. So, I made my main focus loving myself and getting to know "me" a lot better.

I tried new foods and different fashion styles to figure out which ones I liked. I even started going out on "solo dates". I'd get all dressed up, do my hair and make-up, then would go to a restaurant where I'd ask for a seat for one. And I loved it! I also did this thing where I'd look in the mirror and say positive things about myself—to myself. I admit that I had low self-esteem before doing it, but after a few weeks, my self-esteem was improving and it was such an amazing feeling.

Finding myself was the best thing I've ever done. It made me realize that the person I needed the most was *me* and I promised myself that I'd never lose her again.

**The Raw Fact**

Growing up in a toxic family can have a terrible impact on a person, but realizing that your past does not define your future, will save you.

We are hardly ever told this, but sometimes it's okay to be selfish in the sense that it's necessary to put ourselves first. If not, we'd lose ourselves in the process of solely focusing on others. We should be loving ourselves and others, and living our lives to the fullest. But we cannot effectively love others if we haven't learned to love ourselves first. That's the real and raw fact.

<u>Chapter Twelve</u>

## CAREER-DRIVEN

***Dena's story***

When I was seventeen, I came up with a detailed plan on how I would become a millionaire by the age of thirty.

I'd start a business while in college and when I got my Associates degree, I'd get a job (that way I'd earn more money). Then I'd use the money I earned to invest in my business while I concentrated on getting my Bachelor's degree. By the time I would've graduated, my business would be successful and in the ensuing years, I'd focus on expanding. Later on, I'd start more businesses and invest in real estate and the stock market. My goal was to have at least seven streams of income by the time I was thirty-years-old. *Why seven?* you might ask. Well, I read somewhere that the average millionaire has seven streams of income.

I had a plan, but I also knew it wasn't going to be easy. Other kids would be partying, enjoying college life and travelling, but I was willing to give all of that up. I started to watch lots of motivational videos from speeches to millionaires' morning routines. I wanted more than anything to be successful; it was all I ever thought about. So, I worked and went to college, and trust me—it was so stressful. I was waking up at 6:00 a.m. to go to work; getting off at 5:00 p.m.; going to school for 5:30 p.m.; leaving at 9:00 p.m., then working on my business for hours before retiring to bed. I had under-estimated how hard it really would be.

I started having frequent migraines and after seeing a doctor about them, she told me that I was under an incredible amount of stress (which I knew) and that I was pushing myself too hard. In other words, I just needed to take it easy.

I knew I had to do something, so I decided to do simple things like going to bed earlier; treating myself often to something I enjoyed, and meditating. After doing these things for a while, most of the stress was gone. I think I would've avoided the whole situation if I had someone to talk to, but I didn't, so I just kept my feelings inside. Because I was so busy all the time, I rarely got to see or talk to my friends.

The day I graduated from college was one of the happiest days of my life because I honestly hated it the entire time! Being on college campus literally felt like I was stuck in prison and it gave me anxiety just thinking about being there.

Graduation day was also great because it was the day that I quit my job. I had more than enough money saved up and was earning more in my business than I did on someone's job. To be honest, sometimes I can't believe I pulled it off! My plan of being rich by age thirty was going great. I was a twenty-two-year-old college graduate and a full-time entrepreneur. I felt like I was on top of the world.

After college, I was putting in fourteen-hour days. My office (*a.k.a* an empty room I'd put a table inside of) was basically my bedroom as well since I spent more time in there than I did in my actual bedroom. I even thought of making it "official" and putting a bed in there, but figured that might be a bit extreme.

I had two phones—one for business and the other was my personal phone. However, I mainly used my business phone since the people I talked to the most were my customers. It's safe to say my social life was non-existent.

By the time I was twenty-four, I had a six-figure business. Of course, this motivated me to add more zeros on to that number. I opened two more businesses later that same year and when I was twenty-five, I purchased my first property and built my first rental complex. I then used the income from that to purchase two more properties where I built two more apartment complexes.

At age twenty-seven, my first business became a seven-figure success. I realized I'd reached my goal way earlier than I'd expected and it took a while to get over the shock. It was like everytime I hit a milestone, it gave me an intense drive to hit more. At this point, I was hungry and wanted to build an empire.

The following year, I moved thousands of miles away from my family to live in Los Angeles. There, I opened a head office for my first business and hired over three hundred employees.

Over the next five years, my businesses expanded and I had offices in more than ten states in America. One evening, as I was walking to my car after leaving the office, I saw an old classmate. I hardly recognized her because she was "very pregnant". I hailed from a distance, but she waved for me to come over. As I was walking toward her, I realized she was with another classmate of ours. It turns out they got married in California and she was six months pregnant with their second child. The most awkward part of our conversation was her asking if I had any kids. I told her I didn't, then she asked if I had a boyfriend or husband. All I could say was, "Nope. It's just me", then there were a few moments of silence.

When I arrived home, I just sat in the car and stared at my huge house that I was barely ever in and where I lived all alone. At that moment, I took a hard look at my life and realized I was completely alone. The closest people I had as friends were my employees and I was thousands of miles away from my family. I'd spent a lot of my adult life chasing success, but I went about it the wrong way. I was so focused on making money that I'd pushed my loved ones away. I was thirty-six-years-old and had never even thought about having a family. The funny thing is… I've always wanted one, but I guess it wasn't a priority.

Right then and there, I knew I had to adjust my mindset and make some smart changes in my life. I hired a C.E.O., so I could work less, then I visited my family more often and reconnected with friends.

On my thirty-seventh birthday, I was at a club with some friends celebrating. That was the night I met Peter—the man I'd eventually marry and spend the rest of my life with. I felt so complete because I had an amazing career and wonderful people in my life. I wished I'd woken up sooner, but maybe it had to be like this. If it wasn't, I probably would've not met Peter.

**The Raw Fact**

We all want to be successful, but losing ourselves and our loved ones in the process is not the way to go about it. It's great to think about the future and carefully plan for it, but sometimes—to our detriment—we forget to live in the present. There are a lot of career-driven ladies out there who wished they hadn't made some of the mistakes Dena did while heading up the ladder of success. For some, it seems like it's too late because all their youth was spent *chasing the dream* when now being much older, the "dream" doesn't seem to be as important anymore.

If you want to be successful, work very hard at it—give it all you've got—but let there be a balance. You don't have to be a "party-animal", but be deliberate about taking time out every so often for yourself and your loved ones. No matter how much money you make or how many things you can buy with it, you can never buy love and it can never rid you of the loneliness you'd feel after shutting everyone that mattered out of your life.

# Chapter Thirteen

## TRUE SISTERHOOD

Ladies, it's time to wake up and smell the coffee! We are NOT in competition with each other. If you thought we were, you are sadly mistaken. The truth is we're sisters and good sisters don't spend their time trying to compete with one another and bring each other down. Let's be daring enough to set a trend which is to look out for one another, uplift each other and teach each other those things that can be beneficial along life's journey. Let's encourage one another when things look hopeless; extend a helping hand to another female who can use a boost; speak kindly about a fellow female who's not in our so-called clique or "girls club". And let's do what we can to help her along. Include all women in your "girls club" so that together we can empower one another and hold each other's hand. In doing these things, we are loving one another. In the end, isn't that all that matters? This is true sisterhood.

Together, we can be powerful in many ways and in this generation, can set the trend for those who come after us. Too many times, women are busy back-biting one another and bringing each other down by any means possible. That way, we're tearing down the whole mountain until what lies in front of the world is a massive rubble. However, we cannot find true sisterhood if our minds are not receptive.

A major problem in the fight for unity amongst us sisters is our perception of ourselves. How many girls or women have you heard refer to themselves or another female as a "bitch"? Are you aware of what a bitch is? Let me get the definition for you. Oxford Dictionary defines a bitch as a female dog, wolf, fox or otter. Dictionary.com defines it as: a female dog. Catch the drift? Although dogs are wonderful, the word "bitch" when referring to women is used in a derogatory way. It's bad enough when some men choose to address women in that manner, but to hear a woman call herself that and/or other women is not cool. Where is the self-respect and where is it for others? The reason why many women don't show true sisterhood is because of a twisted thought-process that must be straightened out. You are a queen—and a queen is worthy of respect and honor. However, if you don't respect or honor yourself, there's little to no chance that you'll respect others or that they'll respect you. It's a raw and proven fact. You must first tap into and practice self-respect. A good place to start is by being very cautious about what leaves your lips and influences your life. Yes, words are powerful and they actually give direction to your life's journey.

The perception you have of yourself is the place to start. Take a look in the mirror, but peer beyond your physical image staring back at you. Focus on the mental, emotional and spiritual part of yourself (straight into the core of who you are)—your soul. Now, picture yourself—that special entity—as a queen. This takes concentration and focus, but once you get that image and clarification of the true you, can you possibly now refer to yourself as a bitch? I would think not. If you view yourself as royalty (which you are), you'd act like it. Not with your nose up in the air, but you'd walk with grace, with a pep in your step and with a confidence that's alluring. To be called a bitch by anyone would be an insult and nothing less. That's how you need to perceive it. Once the image you have of yourself is clear and you accept that you are indeed a queen (which has everything to do with the amazing fact that you were privileged to be born female), you would choose your words wisely whenever you refer to yourself or address another woman, for that matter.

We are all connected. We may not look the same and each of us are indeed unique, but we share some commonalities that cannot be overlooked. We are life-givers, nurturers, and emotional beings. Even if we're childless, we have the capacity to nurture and to do it in such a way that makes us different from most males. If you happen to have children, whether through blood or adoption, how protective are you of them? We're not known as "Mama Bear" for nothing! When they've done something wrong, how often do you try to deal with it and without telling Dad who might lay down the law a bit stricter than you would? When your child is hurt, whether it's a scrape from a fall or from a failed relationship, won't you move hell or highwater to take the pain away? What about when they're sick? Didn't you sometimes wish you could trade places with them? If you say this doesn't describe you, it doesn't mean you weren't born with these natural reactions and it certainly doesn't mean you can't be this way.

Many times when women's hearts are hardened or they appear "cold", it's because of some issue from the past they either haven't quite dealt with or have dealt with in the wrong manner. If any of us are going to be the best person we can be, we must deal with the pain of the past. We must face it all head-on, then move away from it—for good! There's no getting around that. Living in denial is not helping because in the subconscious, the emotions attached to what we refused to face are eating away at us mentally, physically and emotionally.

As life-givers, that term has more ingrained in it than simply being child-bearers, as not all of us bear children. However, we do have the ability to bring *life* to a household, to a relationship, to a marriage. We are blessed to be able to influence and propel others to succeed whether it be our children, our friends or our significant others. Many women like Oprah Winfrey are positively influencing the world in a major way. We all have that inherent ability, but we must tap into it. Not all of us will be given the world as our platform, but we can positively influence those around us—in our households and in our communities. The older women can teach the younger ones verbally and by example and vice-versa. Yes, the younger girls and women can also inspire the older ones. Wisdom comes in many packages and sizes. Don't make the mistake of closing off your mind to that fact.

Life-giving is not just an asset of ours, it's a duty and responsibility. Whether or not we believe it, each generation is responsible for the next which means that as women, each of us has a part to play in the here and now. That's why it's so important for us to recognize who we are and our self-worth because that is when we'll be able to effectively live up to our responsibility. If we tackle the hindrances, we change the world one heart at a time and what women like Oprah can do on the global platform, we can do in the manner intended for us and still be greatly effective. This is deep, but certainly crucial. There is a reason you were born and a reason you are a woman.

The real and raw fact is *(and I repeat)* that women are *life-giving*, *nurturing* and *emotional* human beings. We were created to love and in order to love other women as sisters, we must, and I stress, *must* love ourselves. We have an awesome duty and responsibility not just to ourselves, but to others. And when we embrace this fact and work on *us*, we can effectively demonstrate and also bask in the essence of true sisterhood.

# Chapter Fourteen

# AVOIDING SELF-DESTRUCTIVE BEHAVIOR

Self-destructive behavior is any behavior that leads to self-harm which can be physical or mental.

Some people have been engaging in self-destructive behavior because they desperately want to be accepted by others. Many think if only they could get into the best physical shape and be attractive to others, then they could feel the way they yearn to feel inside. They either work out constantly at the gym or take diet pills that may or may not be harmful, in order to achieve this goal. However, their obsession for acceptance has made simple habits into a chore; they've pushed themselves beyond healthy limits which, in turn, has done more harm than good.

Others engage in self-destructive behavior by means of excessive shopping; always wanting to stand out in the crowd and sometimes getting material things that they cannot afford. They destroy their credit and put themselves and/or their families in debt all because they want to be accepted as someone special. If only they knew they were special from the moment they were conceived and that they didn't have to take drastic measures to make themselves feel like they were. Many people have lived decades on such an unhealthy emotional roller coaster and still have not achieved that seemingly elusive belief that they are good enough just the way they are and that their value doesn't have to be proven by doing things and *getting things* that can never bring them true happiness.

Others have chosen drugs to hide the pain of feeling unworthy, or repeatedly cut themselves to dull some emotional pain or loss; while others have sought acceptance through sexual promiscuity. All of these actions are self-destructive and in time eats away at the soul—at the core of who you really are.

***Here are some ways that you can avoid self-destructive behavior:***

- Before you act, think about the consequences of your actions.

- Practice self-care: love yourself, embrace your individuality; speak positive affirmations daily (these things were discussed earlier in the book).

- Communicate clearly with the people around you.

- Meditate.

- Stay away from negativity.

• When you are angry, count to ten before you respond.

• Avoid what triggers you; e.g.: certain songs/videos, even people who are a bad influence.

• Learn how to shift your thoughts at will. For example: If something negative enters your mind, immediately focus on something that makes you happy.

Take control of your life and your thoughts. Don't allow life or thoughts to take control of you. This is called *self-empowerment.* When you empower yourself, you won't self-destruct. You will formulate good habits that will benefit you and those around you.

# Chapter Fifteen

# AFFIRMATIONS

**I am beautiful**

**I am worthy**

**I love myself**

**I love my body**

**I am brave**

**I am loved**

**I am happy**

**I am passionate**

**I am peaceful**

**I am powerful**

**I am creative**

I am intelligent

I am loving

I am strong

I am patient

I have a purpose

I am fearless

I am positive

I am wise

I accept the things I cannot change

I am confident

I am comfortable in my own skin

I love my life

I am unique

I am good enough

I am in control of my mind

I am full of life

I am respected and respectful

I am open-minded

I am trustworthy

I am considerate

CONCLUSION

If you've had a similar experience to any of the cases presented in this book, the fact is you know what it's like to not feel appreciated, to feel unloved or not good enough. You may have spent your entire life thinking you weren't beautiful because somebody told you that or based on outside influencers that had nothing to do with you, you came to that conclusion about yourself. You may have successfully moved on and conquered those negative feelings or maybe you haven't. Perhaps you needed the information contained in this book to be a "wake up call" for you. If so, it is our hope that you are able to take what you've read among these pages and adopt them into your life, remembering that you are a queen; you are worthy to be loved, respected and to succeed in life. Also, that regardless of any physical characteristics you may have, you are beautiful simply because you are WOMAN and you were intricately created out of Love.

Live your life and love completely. Every morning you wake up, say something positive about yourself. Use the affirmations that have been listed here and any you can think of that uplifts you as a female. Take control of your thoughts because you will follow where they lead. It's that important. And remember: it's not too late to apply these principles—no matter your age, your failures or what anybody had said to you recently or long ago. As long as you're alive, you can make the rest of your existence meaningful, particularly the way you view yourself and life as a whole, even if your circumstances aren't the most ideal.

Commit to doing the work. Practice makes perfect. You deserve to see the fruits of your labor and in time, you will.

*Love and hugs to every female out there!*

**You are beautiful;**

**You are worthy;**

**You are gifted;**

**You are smart;**

**And you deserve the best!**

From now on, step out of your house with **confidence**—whether you're going to a ball or just down the street to the store. Put that pep in your step, honey! The world has so much to offer you. Indeed, it is your oyster.

*If you're still here, it's for a reason. It means you still have more to do! Use your time wisely, be productive and don't waste it by worrying about the things you can't change. Invest it in those you love and others you can help, so that when it's gone, there will be no regrets.*

**Tanya R. Taylor is a Readers' Favorite Award-Winning Author.** She has been writing ever since she was a child and published her first book titled: *A Killing Rage* as a young adult. She is now the author of both fiction and non-fiction literature. She writes in various genres including: Paranormal Romance, Fantasy, Thrillers, Science-fiction, Mystery and Suspense.

Tanya's books have made Amazon Kindle's Top 100 Paid Best-sellers' List in several categories. Her book *Cornelius,* the first installment in a successful series, climbed to number one in Amazon's Teen & Young-adult Multi-generational Family Fiction category. And *INFESTATION: A Small Town Nightmare* and *CARA* are both number one international bestsellers.

**Mercedes Taylor writes in the pen name** *Tara Tomlinson*. She is a nineteen-year-old Law student and the owner of three online businesses, the first she started when she was just seventeen-years-old. She has been featured in three of the leading local newspapers in her hometown of Nassau in The Bahamas and has been invited to give a speech to a university class regarding entrepreneurship. She plans to obtain her Law degree and to establish more businesses in the future. Mercedes is also the daughter of award-winning author Tanya R. Taylor.

# REVIEW REQUEST

If you found this book useful, please consider leaving a review online at the bookstore you purchased it from. Your honest review will help others to discover it who may also find it helpful for themselves or their loved ones.

Thanking you in advance.

<u>**FICTION TITLES BY TANYA R. TAYLOR**</u>

<u>www.tanya-r-taylor.com</u>


<u>* LUCILLE PFIFFER MYSTERY SERIES</u>
<u>Blind Sight</u>
<u>Blind Escape</u>
<u>Blind Justice</u>
<u>Blind Fury</u>


<u>INFESTATION: A Small Town Nightmare (The Complete Series)</u>


<u>* THE REAL ILLUSIONS SERIES</u>
<u>Real Illusions: The Awakening</u>
<u>Real Illusions II: REBIRTH</u>
<u>Real Illusions III: BONE OF MY BONE</u>
<u>Real Illusions IV: WAR ZONE</u>


<u>* CORNELIUS SAGA SERIES</u>
<u>Cornelius</u> (Book 1 in the Cornelius saga. *Each book in this series can stand-alone.*)
<u>Cornelius' Revenge</u> (Book 2 in the Cornelius saga)
<u>CARA: Some Children Keep Terrible Secrets</u> (Book 3 in the Cornelius saga)
<u>We See No Evil</u> (Book 4 in the Cornelius saga)
<u>The Contract</u>: Murder in The Bahamas (Book 5 in the Cornelius saga)

The Lost Children of Atlantis (Book 6 in the Cornelius saga)
Death of an Angel (Book 7 in the Cornelius saga)
The Groundskeeper (Book 8 in the Cornelius saga)
Cara: The Beginning - Matilda's Story (Book 9 in the Cornelius saga)
The Disappearing House (Book 10 in the Cornelius saga)
Wicked Little Saints (Book 11 in the Cornelius saga)
A Faint Whisper (Book 12 in the Cornelius saga)
'Til Death Do Us Part (Book 13 in the Cornelius saga)

* THE NICK MYERS SERIES
Hidden Sins Revealed (A Crime Thriller - Nick Myers Series Book 1)
One Dead Politician (Nick Myers Series Book 2)

Haunted Cruise: The Shakedown
The Haunting of MERCI HOSPITAL
10 Minutes before Sleeping